David Wevill

Also by David Wevill

Poetry

Penguin Modern Poets 4 (1963)
    (with David Holbrook & Christopher Middleton)
Birth of a Shark (Macmillan, 1964)
A Christ of the Ice-Floes (Macmillan, 1966)
Firebreak (Macmillan, 1971)
Where the Arrow Falls (Macmillan, 1973)
Other Names for the Heart:
    New and Selected Poems 1964-1984 (Exile, 1985)
Figure of Eight:
    New Poems and Selected Translations (Exile, 1987)
Child Eating Snow (Exile, 1994)
Solo With Grazing Deer (Exile, 2001)
Asterisks (Exile, 2007)
To Build My Shadow a Fire:
    The Poetry and Translations of David Wevill
    (Truman State University Press, 2010)

Prose

Casual Ties (Exile, 1983; Tavern Books, 2010)

Translations

Sándor Weöres & Ferenc Juhász
    (Penguin Modern European Poets, 1970)

David Wevill

DEPARTURES

SELECTED POEMS

Shearsman Books

This second edition published in the United Kingdom in 2013 by
Shearsman Books
50 Westons Hill Drive
Emersons Green
BRISTOL BS16 7DF

www.shearsman.com

ISBN 978-1-84861-297-6

Copyright © David Wevill, 1963, 1964, 1966, 1971,
1973, 1985, 1987, 1994, 2001, 2003

The right of David Wevill to be identified as the author of this work
has been asserted by him in accordance with the Copyrights,
Designs and Patents Act of 1988.
All rights reserved.

Cover illustration *Landscape* by Ian Robinson (pen and ink),
Copyright © Ian Robinson, 2003.

Photograph of the author on the rear cover by Dana Lirosi,
copyright © David Wevill and Dana Lirosi, 2003.

Acknowledgements
The author and the publisher wish to thank Exile Editions, Toronto,
Canada, for their permission to reproduce here poems that
first appeared in volumes published by them.
All reprint rights in such poems remain with Exile.

This second edition corrects a few very minor typographical errors
and is presented in a larger format, and with larger type.
It is otherwise unchanged.

Contents

Foreword	8

from Birth of a Shark (1964)

My Father Sleeps	11
Body of a Rook	12
A Legend	14
Water Poem	16
Fugue for Wind and Rain	17
The Birth of a Shark	19
Groundhog	23
Desperados	25

from A Christ of the Ice-floes (1966)

Love-stones	26
A Christ of the Ice-Floes	27
Winter Homecoming	29
Meditation on a Pine-cone	30
Diagona	33
Indian River	34
The Road to China	36
Our Lady of Kovno	37

from Firebreak (1971)

Night / Day	40
Indian Mission, San Antonio	41
Emblem	42
Texan Spring	43
Death Valley	44
Atitlán	47
For Woodwinds	49

Cardinal	50
Three	51
Prayer	52
Memorial I	53
Memorial II	54

from Where the Arrow Falls (1973)

from Part 1: Poems 1–10	55
from Part 2: Poems 10–12	67
from Part 3:	
Song of a Man Thinking About the Shadow	69

from Other Names for the Heart.
    New and Selected Poems 1964-1984 (1985)

Rincón of the heady abstractions	71
Rincón of the soon to be gone	73
The Unapproachable	75
Late Sonnet VIII	77
Late Sonnet XII	78
Villa Blanca	79
Visitors	81
Animula	82
Snow Country	84
Her Seasons	87
Other Names for the Heart	89
Cante Hondo	91
Words for Orpheus	92

from Figure of Eight
    New Poems and Selected Translations (1987)

Premonition	95
Figure of Eight	96
Chinese White	108

Primitive	110
Soleá	111
Assia	113
Full Moon Story	114

from Child Eating Snow (1994)

Baby Upside Down in a Light Snowfall	122
Blue Fur Hood	123
Child Eating Snow	124
Poem Depending on Dashes	127
Old Teacher	128

from Solo With Grazing Deer (2001)

Lamp	129
Landscape	130
Blue Roofs	132
Caravans	133
Railroad Tracks, House for Sale and Clouds	135
The Intimacy of Distance	136
Granddaughter	137
Apples and Apples	138
Nocturne	139
Answers	141
Departures	143
Spring 2001	144
Solo with Grazing Deer	146

Index of First Lines	148

Foreword

Looking through the poems in this selection, I found many I'd forgotten, or half-forgotten, and the voice sometimes of a stranger, or a younger brother. Over time, the contexts have shifted, the loci have changed, though the poems are neither regional nor cosmopolitan. I find that metaphor and image are still my natural tools of composition, and the poems remain rooted in personal concerns. I have moved many times, and resisted moving even more. As a Pisces I have always been of two minds, neither of which seemed sufficient.

I was born in Japan before the war, spent half my childhood there, grew up in Canada, lived ten years in England, and the past thirty-odd years in Texas. My moves, I realize, have been circumstantial rather than planned, and this is true of the poems as well, and my career as a teacher. I am blessed with a living family, but the ghosts remain strong; they live on in the bloodstream, and are present in most of the poems. There is a female shadow in many of the poems, which I'd hesitate to call muse or anima. Nature, too, is a strong presence, though more often an occasion for elegy than for celebration. The poems might touch upon, but do not address, public issues—a shortcoming I regret in an age when speaking out seems more and more important.

Over the years, I notice, the voice in the poems has grown quieter, the syntax has changed, the language has become less energetic and more reflective. But the field I think has remained much the same. It has often been said that one writes the same poem over and over again, but in different guises. I'm reminded of a thought of Roberto Calasso's, from his book *KA: Stories of the Mind and Gods of India*, where he writes: "In the beginning is always something that later gets hidden". It is a genetic intuition that might apply to poetry as well as other forms of life, a germ of first identity that is hidden but not lost in the passage of time.

"…an inner persistence toward the source", to borrow from the poet Robert Duncan. This, I think, is the journey one is making when starting a poem. The risk of failure is always there, but the compulsion seems imperative.

The poems in this selection are taken from eight books dating from 1964 to 2001, the better part of forty years. I owe a large debt of thanks to Tony Frazer, a persistent and invaluable force in the dissemination of poetry in our time. It was he who conceived of this book, and played by far the greater part in selecting the poems. Any shortcoming is mine, as these are my words.

David Wevill
Austin, Texas
2003

My Father Sleeps

Who brought from the snow-wrecked
Hulk of winter his salvaged
Purpose; who came, blind but friendly
By these lines his mouth and his eyes
Have fixed; and without further talk
Taught me at last how to walk,
Until by his power I came
Out of innocence like the worm's flame
Into daylight. What practical need
His patience had, and anger bred
Of disillusionment, has gone with age.
I have this white-haired image,
Arrogant perhaps, and too much the hero
For our friendship's good: Lear, although
Afraid of words as of madness,
Of procrastination as of disease—
A lover of plain-spokenness—
Though not where it hurt, that he could understand.
If I trace the scars in my right hand
They tell me of purpose disobeyed,
Of old and factual truths my head
Cannot alter. And watching him thus
Sprawled like a crooked frame of clothes
In the sleep of sixty years, jaws firm,
Breathing through the obstacle of his nose
A stubborn air that is truth for him,
I confront my plainest self. And feel
In the slow hardening of my bones, a questioning
Depth that his pride could never reveal;
That in his sleep stirs its cruel beginning.

from *Birth of a Shark*

Body of a Rook

God broke upon this upturned field; trees
Wedged tangled and thick as black crotch-hair—
But an eyelid in the field's face flutters,
Winks, blindingly. Whose
Sunrise through that blazing shrub glows
Ram's horns? twin forks of a tree,
Dividing, splitting. And nothing disturbs
These soft tussocks, the woman's one-eyed love.

In the scenery of crushed glass, here,
Among kneading hands of mud, the scoured head lies,
A world seized between sunlit clouds,
Spinning with sense, one eye gone black.
I stare out over my roof of towns,
And shiver off my sperm of wet dog-hair—

Night's claw, where cats couple among
The strict soldiering lupins. As afterthoughts,
My manners brush their teeth into the sink
A cloud keeps my bed, the hot patch kept,
Warmth of armpits and incendiary struggles—
I return where my love gloats and swarms to sleep.

Imagine, if our naked bones
Broke up on these same stones, that freed stubble
Mouth jagged as smashed plastic—
Our nakedness breathes and shifts through warm holes,
Sighs from pricked gaps (the manners torn);
We know our natures and our flaws
Closer, from such uncharitable hunting…

I prise the blue-black feathers back. The beak glows,
Soft at the edges, like an urchin's valve-

from *Birth of a Shark*

Mouth. I know my own violence too.
I feel her gnawing, clinging, flesh-stubbed
Teeth in me, my remembrance of her mouth.
It is a killing but who dies?

I killed it slowly with a lump of flint.
Shot down and left to die, what soft thing jerks
Its pulped head, face, body, nerves
Beak-deep in the pasture mud? I watched
Those last sufferings leave her body too,
Twitching black and rook-supple before
I kicked my damaged violence into the wood.

from *Birth of a Shark*

A Legend

The sinewy nerves of a cabbage now
Contain my head. Its pulse-count
Falls to a trickle, under the icing of hope.

I am more things than a vegetable,
Or a landscape battered blue by March;
I run over them. I perpetrate
Cruelties at their roots. And still they follow
Their needs and ways: burns
Heal in the generations, old wounds grow stony
And bother nothing but the mind.

Through it all, my telltale streaks in the wind
From her quarter. I am more
Than these things. Who would judge my secrets?

So I wake one morning, and tell my legs
Of the difficult journey made
Aghast in the dream. How small I must make myself!
And how great—

With catastrophe! The beating of rain
Eats into the sun's thaw. I have gathered wood
To build my shadow a fire—
Is she female? At lunch I chew my meat
Slowly, wondering if I am vegetarian.

I nibble drily at crusts and become
The whole, huskless grain before an aching fire.
A pride like mine must have
More lives in its hands than one,
And in such generous variety that
The stars seem egotistical. Who would complain

from *Birth of a Shark*

Of the number of swordblades and ploughblades
Through which the earthworm now
Pushes his waste? And still

The deserted, the dead, and the blind go underground,
To weep at these monstrous remains
That never grew in them.

I watch them now;
My altars of fire and sunlight become
Too crowded with worshippers. I go down
Hoping, Eurydice, to find you there.

Water Poem

In this sea I find a lake,
Its white-ribbed waves and grey deep flesh
Drags skeletons up by the hair,
Every wavelet a luminous eyeball.
For boys who loved water, for men who tear at it
Frenziedly, like a fifth wife,
The sea's salt distills
To birth-freshness. But now, when the wind
Drives down hard, and the big clouds turn and heave
Ploughshares of wet grey over the water,
I see through the salt a clear eye
Closed for ever on a night of deep water—
A man's lungs burst with fresh water,
A man's throat choked with salt.

                        Some body that drowned
Would grow that perpetual lull in its cells,
Sweeping and washing with
The eardrum-poised crayfish: flesh
Discarded, the sea's afterbirth—
Freshwater cells and the salt pores tight
As wet drumskins, unwinding with
The sea's time that unravelled Ahab—
The sea's freshwater diet, men and the rain.

In our childhood there was a lake
That changed its cry three times a day, and the fourth
Time was night. Its deadheads rose up
Erect out of the washlight,
Fertilized dragonflies, stove boat-hulls in.
These were incidentals. We knew
That a lake is as deep as the land around it
Allows: as a man is deep,
But dies to that greater depth, sea and the rain.

from *Birth of a Shark*

Fugue for Wind and Rain

We come into a new time; the heavy-mooned
Darkness hangs its orange crater flare
Above the sea.
My beaches are quiet: not a crab
Shuffles to disgorge its load of soft bulk from its outworn
Shell and die
In patterns on the sand. To-night
The wind sickens with heat : late strollers loaf
And stumble over kerbs; and all
Earth's energy's coiled with this soaking sheet wrung
From the insomniac's dreamed sleep of the windstorm.

We come into a new time,
The world and myself: parable of the dog
Who buried his sense of smell with the bone-scraps,
And could find neither.
Consuls, lictors, slaves—
Dipped in Caesar's blood, blood of the fishes;
Men and their knives of rule, manners, lives, hypocrisy
Of bride and groom, ride on
Bloodily to rebirths. In my effort to call them back
I make slaves of everything I see: that ditch
Where wineskin-fat cactuses gripped
The white solid fortress rock,
Where red-back beetles fought and tore at each other's
Strung nerves: in the violence of thunder off the hills'
One rainstorm in a month,—
In our bodies gored by the flame of July night.

Night along the sea promenade,
Black as my boots and finer than hair,
Drifts with the flickering torches of ships towards that far
White mustering of daybreak—

from *Birth of a Shark*

Time of the Greeks and before, the sea, these coasts
A haze of bound chapters now.
Over this nurturing ache of black
Nothing breaks; but is made to know its final breakage plain
And whole as a part
Of the fissure it came from. I look,
And can see no change: but am myself
The sign itself of change in everything: the clean, sharp
Fissure that bleeds the cactus, the deadly
Rote and scrabble of the red
Beetles spitting out their eggs...

Storm draw the water out of me.

This sea has many coasts,
And every inch and brown pool
Is a fingerprint. The gannets come
Plunging, wreck their sight; the sea-salt keeps
The crab-flesh it corrodes ; and the grape-
Avenging Dog-star locks
These fiery lives to the pillows we drown on.
Age has its lovers:
And neither history nor bad experience can ever redeem my one
Fault-finding
First error. I look for the change of light, now
Over this sea: which tomorrow promises only by small chance
To reveal, be re-revealed
Through its weak heart of water, my body, my blood.

from *Birth of a Shark*

The Birth of a Shark

What had become of the young shark?
It was time for the ocean to move on.
Somehow, sheathed in the warm current
He'd lost his youthful bite, and fell
Shuddering among the feelers of kelp
And dragging weeds.
His belly touched sand,
The shark ran aground on his shadow.

Shark-shape, he lay there.
But in the world above
Six white legs dangled, thrashing for the fun of it,
Fifty feet above the newborn shadow.

The shark nosed up to spy them out;
He rose slowly, a long grey feather
Slendering up through the dense air of the sea.
His eyes of bolted glass were fixed
On a roundness of sun and whetted flesh,
Glittering like stars above his small brain—

The shark rose gradually. He was half-grown,
About four feet: strength of a man's thigh
Wrapped in emery, his mouth a watery
Ash of brambles. As he rose
His shadow paled and entered the sand,
Dissolved, in the twinkling shoals of driftsand
Which his thrusting tail spawned.

This was the shark's birth in our world.

His grey parents had left him
Mysteriously and rapidly—

from *Birth of a Shark*

How else is a shark born?
They had bequeathed him the odour of blood,
And a sense half of anguish at being
Perpetually the forerunner of blood:
A desire to sleep in the currents fought
Against the strong enchaining links of hunger,
In shoals, or alone,
Cruising the white haze off Africa,
Bucked Gibraltar, rode into the Atlantic—
Diet of squid, pulps, a few sea-perch.

But what fish-sense the shark had
Died with his shadow. This commonplace
Of kicking legs he had never seen:
He was attracted. High above him
The sunsoaked heads were unaware of the shark—
He was something rising under their minds
You could not have told them about: grey thought
Beneath the fortnight's seaside spell—
A jagged effort to get at something painful.

He knew the path up was direct:
But the young shark was curious.
He dawdled awhile, circling like a bee
Above stems, cutting this new smell
From the water in shapes of fresh razors.
He wasn't even aware he would strike
That triggered last thrust was beyond his edgy
Power to choose or predict. This
Was carefully to be savoured first, as later
He'd get it, with expertise, and hit fast.

He knew he was alone.
He knew he could only snap off
A foot or a hand at a time—
And without fuss—for sharks and dogs

from Birth of a Shark

Do not like to share.
The taste for killing was not even pleasure to him.
And this was new:
This was not sea-flesh, but a kind
Of smoky scent of suntan oil and salt,
Hot blood and wet cloth. When he struck at it
He only grazed his snout,
And skulked away like a pickpocket—

Swerved, paused, turned on his side,
And cocked a round eye up at the dense
Thrashings of frightened spray his climb touched.

And the thrashing commotion moved
Fast as fire away, on the surface of sun.
The shark lay puzzling
In the calm water ten feet down,
As the top of his eye exploded above
Reef and sand, heading for the shallows.
Here was his time of choice—
Twisting, he thought himself round and round
In a slow circling of doubt,
Powerless to be shark, a spawned insult.

But while he was thinking, the sea ahead of him
Suddenly reddened; and black
Shapes with snouts of blunted knives
Swarmed past him and struck
At the bladder of sunlight, snapping at it.
The shark was blinded—
His vision came to him,
Shred by piece, bone by bone
And fragments of bone. Instinctively
His jaws widened to take these crumbs
Of blood from the bigger, experienced jaws,
Whose aim lay in their twice-his-length

from *Birth of a Shark*

Trust in the body and shadow as one
Mouthful of mastery, speed, and blood—

He learned this, when they came for him;
The young shark found his shadow again.
He learned his place among the weeds.

from *Birth of a Shark*

Groundhog

At the tip of my gun the groundhog sits
Hunched in the sun a hundred yards away.
At this range my Hornet's steel-lipped
Bullet could bleed him dry as a star,
As a rag in the pitching drought-drugged field.

Grasses waver and hide. I watch
His shadow's hare, quick at its burrow's
Mouth; the flinch of his rodent hump
Too far to see, like a piece of my eye put out.

No lead gift for a hawk this bead I draw.

Magnetic steel's the moment's only touch
Between us. Though his teeth and scent are sharp
They twitch no warning from the hot bright air.
And I cannot kill, but mark him, fat
As a neighbour safe in his rocking-chair.

Flat on my hips I lie in wait.
Earth beats with my heartbeat, and now
My body's jelly's hardened to take the blow
Of its triphammer weight at the soft exposed
Centre. Imagining it, I retreat—
Wait minutes as his black speck grows
Whiskering through the stalks of Indian corn
To confront me with 'Thou shalt not kill'—
A matter of temperament. No, his fate's
Inhuman, not mine. The riddle is why.

The riddle's this nerve that pecks at my hand.
Scissors to slice my aim's thread now would touch
Terror like a jumping nerve: Zero-urge,

from *Birth of a Shark*

Guiding my right hand and my eye—
Not the will's choice crying unmistakably No.

I fired because confusion made me think...

One spoilt instant's enough to be conqueror.

And now his brown blot melts to its darkest hole,
But I've beaten him there; in the dark, I feel him drop
Slithering past me, wet at the spot I touched.

from *Birth of a Shark*

Desperados

These four lie on a blanket,
A cluster of cactuses hides them from quick
Discovery and the road. Three are grown men,
Fat and moustached, stretched flat on their backs with eyes
Wide and staring, as if the sun
And not bullets had struck them dead.
The fourth, a child, lies closest in the photograph,
Her eyes half-shut with the instantaneous
Headache of lead. Now in this child's face
The crime folds its hands and waits—
Horror-struck. While somewhere in those far hills,
Baked white as the whitest bread,
Black figures with smoking pistols break
A cigarette and share it. Why did she die?
They do not ask now. They squat,
Hands slumped between their knees, waiting the outcry.
And it almost seems the photographer
Was the first one here his silver shutter and lens
Piercing through flies and the blood
Caked on the child's face, gouted on the men's chests.
She was the child of this fat
Official she fell beside; whose round, greedy stare
Somehow smuggled his life out through his wounds
Past the customs of death. He looks surprised—
As if caught in a last act of graft—
And the child beside him, like a sick child,
His graft once protected. Together now
Their tragedy speaks more shrilly than in life:
Her trust, and his shrewd lack of it
Which bought bullets for both on a dusty road;
And the daughter entered her father's life
Without wincing... The other two don't count.
Their deaths enter the hills where the gunmen crouch.

from *Birth of a Shark*

Love-Stones

The three-day blow
Had tossed the lakeshore to its knees—

I found two stones
Lying side by side, just
Touching,
White eggs the sand wouldn't hatch.

But the sun came worrying through clouds
And poured its warmth across the sand—

Not to despair, but to explore
Word against word
The long distance between
Two stones that touch

Without speech,
And at the touching point
A little heat

And after a thousand years
The two stones may be joined

And the sun be forced to modify
The new stone's shadow—

Imperceptibly; because
Witness to witness the legend of the stones
Dies and is reinherited,

Changed, retold
Through no necessity, but
That the stones existed,
That the stone exists.

A Christ of the Ice-Floes

To the trees at the waterline—
Birches, a few elms, a glove of willows, a thorn—
His footprints crushed the snow
And stopped, where the ice was still heavy,
The river's current tearing at its shelves.
Was he deluding himself? Coming here…
It was neither a time of questions nor
Of answers, this in-between season—
Man remaking himself in the image of March,
His testicles drawn in,
His penis shrunken. In the black mid-current
A family of mallards crashed the ice
And swam away downstream… He heard their talk,
Biting the wind, and behind him
The forest dripped, trees
Distilling to earth, roots, leaves,
The monotonous melting. 'Father' he said, 'father'—
Who had imagined, once, his colonies
Of steaming chimneys, earth-proud, God-fearing,
Complacent but watchful, ready now
At the thawing to welcome him home.
The trick was to go away and then return
Later, without promising when,
Without foresaying relief or hope of his kingdom's
Homecoming… He was the word,
They the deed: and the deed deserted by the word
Meant nothing to them: or meant
Too much for their memory of him to outlast his going
And return. They were able—
His people. Upriver his eyes swung
With the turning wind; he saw the big houses,
Shacks, mansions, boathouses, a length of beach,
And the ice-floes ducking downriver like drowned sheep

from *A Christ of the Ice-Floes*

Or so many souls, in the mind,
Starved water, without fish rising...
It was cold, this halfway season,
Wind-chafed skin, the brown earth breaking.
He'd come to imagine his future, not theirs;
He saw now the need of his coming was their myth,
Powerful as the strengthening of each season—
As inevitable, as unbelievable as the first
Bud or flake or brush of puberty—
He took up a stone near his feet
And shied it skittering over the drift ice...
Its brief splash broke him awake...
He felt the water forming round his ankles,
Swaying, rising... he didn't know he was walking
Until the last ice gave, and he stood in the river,
As the stone'd stood—
Less than an instant—,
The brown hair vanished, and the thorn tree drowned.

from *A Christ of the Ice-Floes*

Winter Homecoming

The airfield stretches its cantilever wings,
Its petrified flight of a gull...
Time is before me, blown by the solar wind
Lit by the sun's corona on the snow-sheeted glass.

It is daybreak, heart of winter.
The big jets listen, waiting for their flights.
I watch the blue-veined snowfields bleed with sunrise

Slowly turning my hands to catch,
Reflect, the cold light; asking myself

The way
The messiah comes.

Painfully he comes. Comes now,
As beyond the grey, wolf-shy pineforest,
The ice-shy villas of Montreal,
A million mirrors turn their heads
Watching this bird of departure, hearing his roar
Eventually even to the cross on the mountaintop—

He shakes the blood-pink snowfields,
His red light... green light flashes over the whole
Snow-tortured North—

Touching the snowshoe hare, the arctic fox,
Alarming the businessman sleeping his whisky off...

And I am coming to you this last time
Before the spreading sun has touched your eyes,
Passed on, and left no dawn where your eyes were.

from *A Christ of the Ice-Floes*

Meditation on a Pine-Cone

The pine-cone's whorled
Tongues; woody cavities opening red,
Stubbed, as they touch the air—
These rough hooked knuckles and deserted
Seed-rooms, after the long birth
And sudden drop—
Rain softens now. Rain brings peace over the grass.

II

Here is a city. The sprung cells
Released a people. Now the red money-spider
Hurries through empty rooms,
In and out the skulled eaves,
The firedamp walls. Here is a country—
Levelled with snow to the eye's last hope
And melting trickle. Beyond
Linger the tall parents, twitched by the wind's
Fired coals hissing in the rain…
Leaning out and leaning in,
The unattainable ancestry of the dead cone.

III

Say not dead. For in April, in May
The common blood-drop spider
(Glint of red on her body's globe
Where the sun lies coiled in thread)
Borrows this house for her children.

from *A Christ of the Ice-Floes*

I pick this cone off the grass
And the mother is spilt. Through the dark
Snow-damp rooms her children
Seethe and panic over my hand—
Their ghostly flippers are sharp—
The cone bites back. The cone has another life now.

IV

In Pinecrest cemetery the wind
Snows prevailing north—
In summer it turns; it hums around the cone
And the cone's antennae veer and track the wind
Like a beating heart. The stones
Express their keep in names—
Whole families gathered around one tree
And the pathways glib with pebble-crush
And the mowers working circling swathes
On the green roof of the world where the cones lie—
Crouched cities glazed with webs in the morning-wet
And the name on this stone my own name
As if the cone's earth owned me too.

V

Not yet. Our feet climbed through grass
And cone-stubble to this burial-place—
Death, the quiet pivot.
At earth are the coils that draw me up with the wind,
The living mourners, grateful to live,
Keeping their better selves above the grave,
Burying the unmentionable deep, beyond false touch.

from *A Christ of the Ice-Floes*

VI

But when the sun breaks through the rain
The drying cone whimpers. Words are all you are,
Memory corrects the postures of your body,
Covers the mouth with a hand—
Words inhabit the sprung cone of my head, the cells'
Red spider-mites. And the cone has another life.

VII

I grope uphill and the wind pushes me back
Across a smoking front, breaking the grass like a sea...
I am numb, the cone is numb
In my coat pocket, numb but warm
In the weld of my fist. I carry you over the earth,
Your dwarf-hive a city, a tongued head
At the back of my heart. I carry you over the earth—
Though some would prefer
The adult tree rooted in its four seasons'
Confining coffin. We had no roots, ever—
Our fate was as the cone's I take in my hand,
Grafted to earth, to tree,
Dropping to grass: a pulse only,
Time-blown seeds sharing the wind with dust and rain,
The husk, the house, flung open to the spider-invader
Gnawing her red mark in my hand's possession,
Patient only when the will is buffeted and bleeds.

Diagona*

All day a wolf has chased the sun.
Now, at night, through the double glass
light anoints the snow,
a bitter, grapefruit-pale winter skin.
Blown from the elm branches the snow
holds the branches' last shape
gloved, as it falls. The TV screen
flickers as the wind hunts its wires…
for a moment the mind's
confident riddle is broken. We look at each other,
cross our legs,
worm deeper into sofa and chair,
crack open another can of beer,
watching this act repeated on the screen
by someone handsomer. The wind
husks our lattices, frost
twinkles on the brick and stucco faces—
the germinal and the afterlife of seeds clothes
crash-red bodies on whitening highway verges,
their heads toss slowly in a helpless shock…
Stubborn we are,
to cage our bodies from their victim imaginings,
wincing from the wild
killer's pistol the screen aims at our hearts.
Stubborn, and glad of some peace;
though the wintry earth goes deeper and survives
whatever makes us glad but afraid to live.

*Time of the Iroquois' New Year.

from *A Christ of the Ice-Floes*

Indian River

In February the blind man walked in his maple wood,
Following his dawn and twilight sight;
Enough to see his trees and the snow
With a listening, tapping attentiveness
Not wholly blind, not midnight-blind.
"Go deeper…" urged the trees. "You will find
False faces in the maple woods: masks tortured from dreams,
    carved by hand,
By our craftsmen." I walked in the wood at the break of winter,
I edged from tree to tree, each tree
Repeating my shadow, until the whole wood
Was one tree with my shadow leaning, peering around it
Like a bole-growth. I was alone,
The only hunter in the wood;
My feet left wet eyes behind in the softening snow
And I gathered back my sight. I closed my eyes,
And leaned against a tree whose bole was a round, hard
Beating tumour; and I saw
(Hugging the tree)
The carved, painted face
They'd chosen for my punishment
And cure. It had red, wind-drained eyes
In a birch-white scowl… a grin
Twisted the jaw to the left, and the bent nose
Broke it in half like a crimsoning sunrise
Banked by a low hill… It was nothing on earth
I knew; for fear of what I'd become
And what I'd feared to see was not in this face—
This was a stranger to man, dog and dream.
"Go deeper…" said the trees. Then I paused and thought,
If this is the creature I thought me, the man
Without hope, then I have been cheated;
For he is no part of my body, this skew-jawed

from *A Christ of the Ice-Floes*

Skull of grief. He is the crime of another,
An idiot's craft, or a murderer's. What my skull
Suffers, tracks in the snow, has no face—
And I opened my eyes and examined the mask.
I stared, and staring forgot what was in me that stared
Back, and took the black tree-stumps
For a council of elders squatting in judgement around me,
And gave every tree my shadow
And wove this mask from the winter-light in their branches…
And my eyes which had opened too soon
Nipped shut with the maple-buds. I stood in the wet
February wind, hugging the tree whose touch
Had given me sight, briefly, of the whole wood and the hills
And fields my blindness had entered…

Now the false faces melt away
In a slow, silent dripping.
The snow dreams its skin away, then its flesh, then its ice-bones
And the bones' marrows of frost—
And my bones put on what the snow discards
Now, in the earth's time of indecision,
The year's uncertain quarter, when the master of life plays his
        game of chance
With the inert spirits of ice and stone,
To win back the green
Good growth over the whole earth.
There is no further sacrifice…
Blind, I have come at last
To the diamond heart of blindness, which is sight…
Then the trees blurred, the fields and hills went dark.
But the blind man could remember his way through the wood.

from *A Christ of the Ice-Floes*

The Road to China

(for Nathaniel Tarn)

To have reached this state
Of waiting, like a stomach for its food—
A high grassland where the wind
Has no beginning or ending,
But just bursts headlong or lies coiled
In the yellowing undulating waves,
Between mountains dry as knuckles dipped in brine—

This valley's passage
Smells of old migrations to cities
Never begun or named. Windburn's
The speed and shake of this old bus
That carries us; the old road north
To China winks under the sprung floorboards.

A man with a black, a woman with a white
Cock, sit together—
Tomorrow is New Year's day.
Every village and cluster of shacks
Opens a moment of memory
On this outward homeward journey.
This is the end of nowhere; out of the mist
Came man. Somewhere in this open, toothless country
One man returns, accustomed to being alone—

A hunter dressed in black
With a bow and arrows and a bloody hare;
A white man with a map,
A sketchpad, and a homing thirst for space.

Our Lady of Kovno

They had crucified a woman;
She was still warm, though the breeze was cold
On the windows lungs and eyes of the square.
The townsfolk turned away and wound their scarves
Tighter in the lime-cold light.

She has no mother,
She is still;
The soldiers come and lift her cross
Over the cobble roads where pink
Sunset puddles blink;
Her figure is gross, flesh to the wooden spine
Where her head hangs down, the long hair trailing red
Over redder eyes: so red
Her hair, they called her Fire-girl, she was loved
Loved, though a virgin, and her sister homely.
They carried her through the streets
And dug her cross a root in the field—
Naked she hung in a blear of dusk, on the cross
Frost-hard. Her shadow looped
Across the fresh-ploughed furrows;
And at such an angle they planted the cross
Her hair hung down to the ground…
The soldiers went away; but one
Stood watching her, with his helmet off—
Holly prickled in his hair
Where sweat and the bristles fought for air.

From their holes in the earth, without lights
The red ants caught her smell, like the sea;
They followed the threadlets of blood
Up the eyelets of air, lacing themselves
In lines and clusters, licking wounds
Which were never theirs to fear or mourn.

from *A Christ of the Ice-Floes*

The brittle armies kissed and passed
The formality of the soldier's boot—
He let them pass; but as the sun went down
With a scuff of disgust he thinned a few;
The ants made a ladder of her hair,
They pieced it out among them, strand by strand
Life crawled back to the girl,
While a scarecrow played
In a nearby field
With a flock of crows.

The soldier with his helmet in his hand
Wandered off around the field.
He trailed his hand along the fences,
Feeling the electric chill of the wires
Whiten his skin; they sang as he scraped his nail
Sirening over the broken grass
Where spiders hunted past their webs…
He grinned and talked to himself:
A mother is safe in her son,
His life unwinding leaves her free for care,
And himself, free, to give his love elsewhere
Than to the cold refusal of a full moon
That blues his helmet and phantoms in his hair.

At the rooted cross a rustle,
Puzzle, a babel of orders,
Falls with a husking sound
Down flanks and through the moonlit genitals
Of the ants' earth… The cave is found.
Quiet… Her body seemed to move.

The soldier returns, unslinging his gun, to finish the
                                          beginning…
The shot spins outward, life comes gently back.

from *A Christ of the Ice-Floes*

Now she is twice dead.
The dark has taken her body.
Ants twist and change their grip,
Ants crofted in the season of reproaches,
High times and furtive fires—
Our lady of pins
In a dry sweat which will not break or open
To any crying comfort…

Ladder-lost, the ants
Buckle and fall: the shot sends panic in.
The creature moon comes up
In solemn stealing; ants carry her blood to their holes
On tiny shrill bobbins. The hour of her death
Crosses from plain to hills; the marshes sing,
A steel helmet buckles the soldier's skull.

from *A Christ of the Ice-Floes*

Night/Day

As dream corrects
the facts of daylight
what cries in me

is no bird
          but some chirping nerve
nested in fear
scrabbling at the fly-screens—
                    'sickness unto death'
in the black
January night

            But the good
body returns
          unbroken
edged like glass
            falling through years
without air

to irrigate a desert
make drinking water from the sea

calms itself
          by numbers
through each of which passes the cell

of a baby's first eyes

widening
to ask
and find

from *Firebreak*

Indian Mission, San Antonio

Chief Seattle never knew
his city
      but said, the dead never die
we are the ghosts of the old land

the burnt-out motel
      the flowering garden of wrecks
are failures of the
front-brain

      So it might have been
Victorio or Cochise who burnt the city in '89
ghosts of the dead
      buried but unappeased

each with his spear
in the side of a timber christ
      too weak to move

The lovely missions were dead
dead from the start
      If this one lives
it is through the tensions of ghosts
who never knew each other's hearts
      or could tell
substance from shadow

the dark hidden tree-grain
the crippled façade of saints
      gone blind in the sun.

from *Firebreak*

Emblem

A man's incandescent skeleton between my eye and the sun.
The atoms burnt through it, a bare, charred heat for
silhouette.

Noble words a smoke ring of flame.
Rhetoric a whisper light years beyond things known.

That gap in the pelvic bone where his race created itself
Those eyes which saw through time images of god and reason,
gone.

Pestered now by meteors, some malarial, others with stings
like horseflies.

Hells Angels are roaring through space. Smoking rubber in the
glass-clear cold airless well, where no sacrifice feels
the black knife slip his heart.

A bare, charred heat for silhouette—
Go, go, filaments, go, of the burnt skeleton.

Lose no sleep over this dream of re-entry into the condom of
daylight and dust. Here the moon's vulva opens. The Sea of
Tranquillity is a dripping cave where blind shell creatures,
colourless, crawl.

In the clear cooling pool the skeletons will harden again,
both male and female.

We wake washed in the sweat where all seas meet.
Bone to bone, our breath sifting through our ribs like wind.

from *Firebreak*

Texan Spring

Headlights in the mirror on a lonely road
frost-still in the warm moonlight

I begin to wonder who my killer is
crawling through deep, dry sand in the craters of
                                    my footsteps
on a bottom of solid glass
                         skidding, searching past
the light-stabs
in the heart

No one, love
just distance
            The high beam with a warning light
and a horizon of dulled silver
where trees pray eternally to the winds
                          lapping the sea at their roots
inland
so far from water
the engine sucking us on

As I am
and as you are
flesh a time-bomb, acorn packed with fire

weasels in their chimneys

solid beef digesting in the rancher's gut.

from *Firebreak*

Death Valley

desert fingers
counting beads, old
spark plugs

her hair
brushes my feet, sifts
like spiders

the long knife in my hand
turned on me
    turned on you

        you

we
know you, you
filed the flesh from my bones
give it back, I
sign my checks in your
blood but
where
    is the in-
terest
you
owe
me

I
looked for
America, let
America come and get me

from *Firebreak*

girl at my feet, go
KILL
my voice flat in your eyes

one life will atone
for every ruined pore in my skin

the pigs
must die, the poor

vomit air

inherit God

        I
am the son
of man,
in the manger you broke me, turned

my cry into words
my touch to trust

all my women, you
blind as to day or night, assassins
with burnt-out eyes

        they will
kiss you
as none have kissed me

as the snake
kisses,

have sucked
my poison
to spit it into your blood

from *Firebreak*

through lips
cracked, so they will
die too
         yes, they will
find you

whoever

my forty days

in whatever
bed
denied
me

by
the
cross

from *Firebreak*

Atitlán

Do you hear this my friend
down there

where the stars call to the sun—
        jaguar, prowls the night
                without shadow

your blood is the river he tracks
from the water-void
        came animals and plants

and man created from mud
        to mud returns

and men made of wood without minds
        destroyed by slash and burn

then flesh—
frail, but of flesh
      made, they melt
in the black rains and floods of the long year

This whisper
keeps the potency of time,
to hold all possible but that which
                        dies in you
of long absence

or, returning to find
the place just as you left it

a bird, a lake, the profile of three mountains

from *Firebreak*

afraid your breathing might anger
the spirits of welcome and death

This is your birth place

You come with clean hands, whom

the flood waters
            drowned

now
grain
revives

In the *Bardos*, to catch the moment when
                        breath dies, breath returns
be patient

listen, don't speak

from *Firebreak*

For Woodwinds

The dry wind ticks in the leaves
The coral snake has left his hole by the water pail
The days climb to a hush
oven noon, and at night
the hidden river leaves a lake in the cup of your belly
where
we dabble like children, lights out
to the small wild noises in the grass
and the dead eye of the gun in the bedside drawer

        II
Some mornings
the sea returns. Our valley of air
alive with sunshapes, shed scales
solders our lungs with the plumb pressure of tons
                            of dark water
No life
    no appetite
But sap drips from the sun into our eyes
                          staining the dust
The cardinal high in his tree
warns of the snake's return

        III
Juniper green on electric blue
enduring while the first leaves fall
and the road subliminal, grey
grainy film of a dead river, goat bones, glass
glitters through dust
                More dead
and many wounded. They cry for time
to tell us what to live for, not to die for—
the old who would take us with them over the river,
lacking the blood we drown in.

from *Firebreak*

Cardinal

He comes in the night between us
the red bird of blood
cocks its tail

                We live
for years in the shadow of one night
knowing
        afraid to know
        why do you ask
                what
contempt makes me answer

The sun shallows in the juniper wood, I
sing to myself
          I shave with words
I eat a red-eyed breakfast egg
you spill the shower over the floor

Now can we begin as the sun drums in the leaves
thinking of time and the false role of the mind controlling it
more substance
than essence

                that what the red bird asks
is the death of us both
and the life of us both

so we may return
hand in hand
walking among thorns

knowing that where our feet touch is the earth
knowing that where our feet touch is ourselves.

from *Firebreak*

Three

I have known three healers
    one, a dead woman
    nearer than anyone
she left to inhabit a tree, under
        the snow I will not meet her
not now

Another was a man
      a greying haired child
   whose vanities were small, his love
a need of love
     bewildered by the world
he loved and feared

You are the third, the one of pure chance
   my wife
      by being no more
than you are. May autumn and the night
        winds cool your fever, now
quiet house
     green blanket
sleep.

from *Firebreak*

Prayer

In the absence of father or god
bless this son

That his eyes will know the details of our lives one day
that created him—

not in the white bitter light
of the empty temple
                wind, stone or myth

But in the bargain
he must make with his heart
to free himself of all fears not his own
                        not kin to his cry

That his temple be filled
with people and beasts
he can trust without taming

That the horns and water of his birth
guide him through the two worlds

belief in self
belief in things

And finally, give him the nerve
to face his own failure
                the darker face
behind the face in the mirror

which is his substance, all else being ghost.

Memorial I

In a time of mock funerals and
pagan prayers for the living,
your death was real.

When there is nothing to mourn but
the future, how can we go on
laying wreaths at your feet?

You spoke of love; but the World
Collective, the collective word
would never understand. You spoke of love,

O, the hole in the breath
like a blessed egg, stillborn
with blood in its eye. You were a winter fury

cursing the lovers
your cold
drove together for warmth... Pity

the dead telephone
whispering in your ear
stories of others; and the sun

trying to enter through your frosted window
gave only a bright cold,
a vivid shield of hell.

After you died
they lied about your beauty;
the sun melted everything into the sea.

And they will go on casting your bones
relentlessly, in the wines of many thanksgivings,
until the living find your dying words.

from *Firebreak*

Memorial II

I visited your grave
too often in dreams
while you were still alive

Now I do not want to touch
the real body and the real grass
see the real trees

        Because
your voice will begin to describe
the leaves, the ladybugs
roots as they are
        the germ of wind
that reaches you
flowers, your neighbours' names

the same voice
that claimed and exclaimed so often
such things, your eyes
        quicker than mine
            still quicker than mine

Where the Arrow Falls

FROM PART 1

1
The top of your head is still open
fragile, hearing whispers of the sun

your teeth are early and strong
your birthmark grows
a rose, in the small of your back

your eyes are smoky and dark
the lashes longer than ours

your rage
knots you so
I can't untie you

all in all you're a fine one
your strength in Leo but jammed between
Aquarius and my fish

soon you'll be a year
our trees are full of owls
our chimney full of young swallows

fire and water and air
and the earth is yours to grow on

meanwhile you have no friends

2
I buried the dead
baby rabbit

found under the cedars
under the cedars

it lies in the ash-pit
flattened by rain
perverse blue of the flies
has gone to haunt another wind

my daughter, blind
to what small life
death can happen Here is a mind

of daybreak and sunset cliff
and an acre of trees
give shade in place of water
Here I learn my time is longer than suns

that, by seeing, by
giving I return
through the back ways of god dragging
my heart like a smashed placenta

sticks leaves dust
out into the open, as
the rabbit trailed its—

break me, I say, break me but do not
scatter the parts
they were a long time growing they
learn to love, painfully, at the end

3
For the Sangre de Cristos
where they appear
fifty miles before the eye can see them

—the eye, blind
from desk and midnight lights   I happened on Cortes
lying under a piñon tree
muttering 'Land, my land'

                Here
his children come
come, before they are broken
or come, by being broken
to break against the sun or the long moon
drying her vulva among the pine needles

Dark night
her vigil
kept by skunks

                or her vigil kept
by angels
lashing their wings to the treetops
each tree a halo pointing to blood dawn

No   no crucifixion
no more crucifixions
man of blood

the mountain breasts are full of milk
milk of black and the soul a solitary tree
for the panther, for who moves
softly here   One among us

or us
in the figure of One
so the sky is once again the jay's nest
and the worm flies in its song

from Where the Arrow Falls

4
Hurt
by our hurt

because we could not
share or be her

a hole
where her body had been, now
imagining it
like scatterings of salt

needing an ocean to
be...

        what is
the whisper that heals

from our dandelion lives plucking
their promises, petal
by petal

—I have seen the bone too,
I ran, being afraid

believe us   there is death in it
and whatever life is there
may be yours, not ours

but   because we could
not, what

is, is,
and there you were

without

and here the crows attend you
our smiles like flashes of tin could not defend you

more
than the earth

5
the candle fixed in a black room
will seem to move
left and right

under the delusion there is
an American Voice
explanation, eating the past
prediction, feeding the future

classical mechanics
got us to the moon… theories
evolve, and are incomplete…

if Nature is the set of all
observations… if

theories are instruments
for making predictions about
observations, the

cool sudden death of the mountains

had you no faith
in the sun's return… who
wills him to suffer, and her

we are still a great way from that star
of new man, and
despite these visions

from *Where the Arrow Falls*

matter screams under time

as these hills of Mexico
grind an old man's drunken tears to dust

and the yellows the blues
the gold the crimson
eat out the heart from my figure of night

January 1971

6
His look, they said
would melt mountains

the mountains are still there, the
ghost of Crazy Horse
still dances visions, stone

impenetrable stone
keeps nothing out

and this poet gets his bang
from repeated annihilations
      falling through time like a stone
to the
one
word

absolute

importance
is nothing alive
the air, before and after man, so pure
a stone never carved

from *Where the Arrow Falls*

it is wistful to play at God

and murder the living in your dreams

7
hero must break with his mother, be
pure energy there-
after. So
in a dry summer
the cedar tree becomes a torch… pouf!
And his words, dishonest, because partial
(as Mao is a functional lie) must
                     free him from gravity
to complete
his *physical* vision, in transcendence

no cat can be a hero
being too lithe in their dance

there's fear in the cardinal too
his red precedes the jaybird's blue
and still, the foetus with two legs
wingless, is the beggar

    I lay and slept
    the hour of my birth
    dark as the stone's throat
    crying into flower

    purple that
    of the unborn eye
    moving around me

    night of the people I'd known

from *Where the Arrow Falls*

love of their unknowing
in this tomb of insolence
crying one name

the poet, the poet's wife
up a long tunnel of twisting water
born before me, after me

lilies of rain
suddenly all over
child-white in the wind that breathed them

under, down
dark gentians toward
the night unborn

dry-mouthed, I rise from my mother
to say her life will bloom again
is not to know that

or she who wrote the poem about
the small dead deer, crying
to her words like a child to her dolls

have no country, want none

is all a film, here
broken, there melted, by
too hot a light… or run too
slow (for effect) to survive
a second or third showing… the sun
that burns away all permanence… kills

what
can replace
the centre. I speak of the heart. These words

from *Where the Arrow Falls*

(heart) returning in their simplicity through
the trail of breakages of a long ago series of
years (dead in exile). Now
intermittent as news of Vietnam, repressed
wanting to know no more.

Caring, unspeaking

a house
broken of its mother

who is to time
what seed
to the apricot tree

was.
      Gesar of Ling
tumbled his flaming horse from the clouds
of heaven, came

the way of the nagas,
killed monster
              returned. Now heaven

is throated with jets…
the hero on wings carries a hundred souls

as Jesus rose in epiphany
over Dorval
              that winter, or seemed
in the snow-light
someone real:
              more mother than man

And I cannot move forward from these
not to your love, though I love you

from *Where the Arrow Falls*

must try my self against stones
or clawing from anus to mouth
repeat the journey I slept
slimed with my own birth

at the edge of dawn, where sun breaks
and the keen pain of the knife

cuts twice

8
At night or just before dawn
dogs in the valley
baying, up the loose stone road
               invaded our hill
a deer? light hoofs
broke the woods' edge
before the wild night mouths
               that broke my dream
melted to echo
the nightmare
               the blood chase
hungry, always hungry
and the bones of the hills glowed
in the afterlight
               the river
under a red unrisen sun
or a red unsetting moon
               in the small hours
when time returns
and the stone breasts of the hills
suckle the deer to their deaths
               or to mine: foretold by the heart's
hoofs leaping
the loose stone road
breaking the woods' edge—

from *Where the Arrow Falls*

deer-self, deer-self!
             ahead of the dogs
all windows open like eyes
             and the stars closed
knowing now
not archetype or dream
but the breaking lungs and heart—
and the forest alone is safe—the forest alone!

9
Somewhere
there is a woman trying
      to teach herself her self

do you say you love her
all the doors
slam on a single hinge

             Ophelia
where are you
I have your hair-ribbons
      not mine, not mine

I have a date with my father
all gifts come and are taken away

they dragged the pond
they found her

ever since then her death has been
a vision, her smile
      like a pained cross
asking
for water
more water

or is it blood

from *Where the Arrow Falls*

10
There is no equality among those
who suffer. Tones come through
into the bones of the ear, we

hear crying, the
depth of the crying is unknown but
as light changes, we feel it:
the light before rain
               the light after rain

Love
can not redeem this. Torn
from its light, the eye
knows nothing but pain,
though the light is pain, you
could not touch the pain
in your daughter's eye but

find a jungle. Those
who must live, cannot live
easily. What breaking point—
when the sun spread its
talons and fell
on her playroom: fire
feathers blood her father's eye

We must be
fanatics even to breathe. The
quiet ones more so. Cold
as the sharp-shinned moon over
the cedars. It
is alone.

FROM PART 2

10
I have built you
nothing, but
our cells know a difference in winds

in touch
a danger

I prayed
to a warped cross, now
I stand half broken, heal me

our cells will melt and close

now is the sun, our moment, given, whole

11
To see it all fresh
forget

bury the bones
then try and find them

hard
harder than death

I am afraid of innocence and
I cannot remember, night
my duty to dream
smells of the wet cedar

my book reads itself
my house is watching me

music out there: rock of the storm
home has eyes
        wind smells of cities
you

forgotten things
drift up in the light
fish-heads without bodies
with living eyes

my duty to dream, not sleep, not
ease like a snake into the hole
of knowing, without eyes

and you are watching
your skin is a number of years
a song I know and don't own

a poem to be found

12
Between midnight and daybreak
seven times for my sins
staring the different winds into their cradles
        owls, nightbirds, cats
the faces I know and do not know—

betrayed by my silence
I think of you now: you burn with me
in this foresleep, before taking your masks and roles
into dreams I cannot control, where
        you triumph or die—
and leave me a husk clinging to a tree

I imagine a better world, larger
a place where the hurt

from *Where the Arrow Falls*

smile over each others' cradles: dwarf, giant
        twins, the without arms or legs
ones, fat lady and rubber man, Ralph
the man with elephant's legs, the bearded lady—
a family circled by fire
but spared by the other-killing fire

so my head will empty itself
for its own sounds to enter:
the Fool coming late to his hands, an effigy
        of dried shit and straw, that
walks, talks, composes poems
that enter through one eye and out the other
so, in a perpetual circle

adobe man, lost on his own plains
a miracle of nightly resurrection and
daily sleep: Wakdjungkaga, between one birth
        and another, eating his own body, his
night confused with his day: no
enemies, no friends, no god but error

as even the stones   fitted to one another

FROM PART 3

SONG OF A MAN THINKING ABOUT THE SHADOW

I was born within you
I wanted out
I got out

you were my mother
my father
I hate and love

from *Where the Arrow Falls*

you do not exist

you are the eyes
of my children
I do not see my children's eyes

I am the world
in sunlight
I do not see the dark world
in my children's eyes

I do not see you

I see you through others
who found you,
her, dead men
and women

they are not part
of my house
my house is world

the tree must live

I have gathered these voices
against you

they are not mine

that world survive

in me

from *Where the Arrow Falls*

Rincón of the Heady Abstractions

Densities: a summer in the country
like other summers in towns
measured by one light or another
that comes or refuses
reek of old earth. This

corner has no exit. If I remember
it is satisfaction of remembering & not
even a body or face to go
under for, strings in my hand
vibrating still with earth's winds.

Orpheus is too old to meet his question.
Above & below there are greater
certainties than love
remembered, a person. Blood
hardened like an old cat after many wars
now stretched out asleep in the sun.

In the country we learn silence
but among friends we are too talkative,
our gossip is old, what
news we must invent. We are painkillers.
We kill for pain & kill the pain
of those things we kill.

In towns this summer the country becomes
whatever age it wants to feel:
the spirit of independence, freed
by choice to choose lies. Lakes
edged by spruce & fir will always be backgrounds.
What happens up close is the perigee
of insatiable alternatives. One by one

from *Other Names for the Heart*

they cut the strings of the song
& the song's replaced by noises that create
their own winds. In this garden
in this slum

we return to ourselves again
in memory. Where have they gone
the man & the woman who fled
terrified before the fiery angel & had

to learn to build fires & make new words
for things they couldn't love.
They were our type, not noble or heroic but
pressed to keep what they'd lost,
remake it with hands, in the smallest possible
image, themselves. & this

corner has no exit. Remembering
may seem one but is false, false
densities, narcosis of sounds of words in
summer thunder. Measured by the old light
one is pale as a fish & not yet
born. & those who confuse their times
remember nothing but what it is like not to be.

from *Other Names for the Heart*

Rincón of the soon to be gone

(For David Moorman)

Banded together again
here, in our now grassless yard—
the rough winterworn brown of occasions
like this—we talk
of unwritten poems, & the earth turns,
minute animations of friable soil
shaken by chainsaws. Wind
parts the cedars, & we imagine the deer
no longer with us, grass gone to the sun,
fencelines opening & closing
restlessly, as strangers make their plans
& are heard of or never appear except
a few more trees have gone. You
our old friend, familiar with the
guest room: this is your house too
where nerves can rest, though ours
aren't easy now & the place
has got out of hand—
unimaginable repairs & so little time
even for these words. We wish we knew how
to be inert & at peace, or
leap those fences & heal them with energy,
that light successful touch no thing can feel
when properly mended. We sit
here where our shadows have always lived
& talk. Soon one must move, some
story begin, arbitrarily, at its first word
& continue on as the wind takes it
faithful to its helplessness without
the signature of the oak or periwinkle
to guide it. So it will
go. It is spring, yet there's this

autumnal drift backward seven years
to a time of more credible waiting
for that war to end which is now just beginning—
blood, then & now, human
red or sap green: the old infection of choice
the same, the ways
both more open & closed. This is
peacetime, we tell ourselves. A time
for children or for lonely energies
to happen in themselves. The tree buds are
still hidden, uncertain: as in dreams
the clues keep generating new darknesses
we stumble on. The horizon of going
is never real enough, but many
pass into eclipse as talk leads us there
& beyond. Somewhere far away
in a city whose streets happen in memory
a table is being laid for your meal tonight.

The Unapproachable

...the vague, the particular no less vague...
   —William Carlos Williams

The cure as with a flower is to water the root,
be gentle, precise in whatever you
can afford to give, what it wants.
The crown of lights it resembles are offices
far into the night
                    numbers giving birth
to new images of the future surrounding you,
and the bridge, the between, stretched
precariously tight from half
to half of what wholeness. Yet

the sun has never watched us,
nor the moon.
Paul Klee lowered the stars
until they hung too huge above our simple roofs,
and a woman turning to a man returns his key
with thanks but regrets. How grave the time would seem
without the jokes we're forced to make of ourselves
suspended like this, as we are,
searching the floor for a lost eye
without which it is hard for me to see
your hurt.
              And the elevators dream

of going beyond, of lifting themselves high
above the layers of rain, or plummeting down
below the water-thirst of flowers
                    which in your hand
are ghostly smells, colors the night can't give
to anything other than numbers on a screen

from *Other Names for the Heart*

as we, to meet ourselves, approach
a mirror placed to make the room seem larger
and are suddenly caught in a smile
both true and false, as the light changes
subtly like a deer running through woods,
but reminding us of blood, and how we tremble now.

Late Sonnet VIII

Always suspect the stranger
but give him a roof, a bed, whatever he needs
to cut your firewood. Offer him blood to drink
and he'll open his heart

to the story you were telling
when he entered. In the firelight his eyes
remember: the autumn nights were cold.
The woods grew shadows no light could open.

He watches the firelight play on her arms
like shadows in a brown stream. The
house had no mood. Sometimes lately

a bird you can't identify has flitted close
and sung from the branches of his hands.

He leaves us touching ourselves.

from *Other Names for the Heart*

Late Sonnet XII

Then seeing it was still alive
we put it in a jar where we could watch it
day and night. Wind and the seasonal rains
browned out the hills, staring through glass

the world seemed to grow older, grew
its colors inward, the beauty there
but gone. I read my daughter's essay and noted
a gift for heightened feeling expressed

as a wish to see us as we'd like to be
angels carved from driftwood
smelling of bodies in love. Delicately the light

steps over us who are
temporarily fallen. When we get up again
we leave these shadows as reminders of where we have been.

Villa Blanca

The dark table where my ancestors ate
is here with us. Two white dogs
guard the entrance to the patio
while the fire on the mountainside at night spreads toward us.

A day spent among birds. Dinner
is talk of another kind, soft ash, fatigue
& America tuned in. The roof is for stars,
the deep slope south & west is where the Pacific begins

beneath our shoulders. Like ones standing in water
we are the mountains. Tomorrow the same &
then home, cutting the fine edge of our journey
along exactly the same line, backward. To

go at last in whatever direction
time tells us, telling us nothing else we can
hear. You are my friends & we all matter greatly
to someone or some idea whose

hidden solitudes need our voices: fire, child or star
confers on us the permanence of the
passer-by, the ones who have been & are about to
leave this table in the mountains as

the fire spreads closer. My ancestors
have cleared away the plates & we're
tired, our words fail us. There will never be a
city here. Our words are too particular, our

ideas shaped by dead names & forms
that call us back to imaginary beginnings
whose pressures remind us of birth, of
these ones born again in us to serve us & dismiss us

from *Other Names for the Heart*

into the question of nightfall & distance
murmuring "time". When we're alone tonight
we will have nothing to talk with but our bodies.
They are this geography, the sierra's superficial bones.

Visitors

(For Christopher Middleton)

Where there were houses there is grass.
What we missed were the shadows
the sun crackling off
painted metal. A few thin trees.

We say we miss that, but the
photographs had it wrong, the latest
evidence shows a family no one remembers
posed in front of a lake

before a low sun
cutting into their eyes.
The shadow of a tree just touches
the man's left shoulder. The woman

leans down to speak
to one of the two girls. The
dogs that run everywhere looking for water
left prints on the muddy valley floor

which have dried. Something went wrong
with the mathematics, with the camera.
There is nowhere to settle here.
Nothing to settle on.

I scrape a bent, rusty nail
on a stone, to see if the metal will shine.
They walk their ponies back up through the grass
that covers the hill. They do not look back.

from *Other Names for the Heart*

Animula

> *We have all become people according to the measure in which we have loved people and have had occasion for loving.*
> — Pasternak

If in your confusion
you could have seen the future
as other than death, as
what it might have been
for your left hand to have begun
perfectly writing the characters
of an unknown language, older than memory

so that the sun, seen clearly as the sun
not just as light, broke
inside you, without the pain of fire
and you were made new, newer than
anything you could remember
ever, of your past

and the man beside you, the woman
beside me, were both one, one
like the deepest vowel, so
that life and death were one sound
and what you had done and what I had
not done seemed only the shame

and pity of uncompleted gestures,
then... Ana, we asked
what happened to your friend?
My friend gave up.
Were you too difficult to love?

But there is no world without pain
without pain no world.

from *Other Names for the Heart*

The inner sun
burns in Cancer

white cold flakes arrested in their
fall to earth. Body

is only body, warmth and cold
not opposites but of the same memory

appetites, the old old hunger
like a warning, like a star.

Mind feeds on mind. Then what is matter?
What are the earth signs? Mind feeds on flesh.
Its hunger enters dreams, it
prowls and resembles an animal
but is mind. To go
and not come back. To
go and not come back.
To go and not come back

I have no body.
I have no body's body.
I am neutral like the sea.

The sun touches this other face
which is your skin, your death.
Beyond this are
the uncanny possibilities of ignorance,
innocence, the sea-bird's cry heard
all night in the girl's ear
repeating and repeating her new name.

from Other Names for the Heart

Snow Country

(For Avanthi)

Kawabata talked about
the "roaring at the center"
deep in the mountains when snow
has covered them. This
is the sound of distances made
heavy, and bare of all details
between your blood and nothing.

Early in the day when things wake
listening, to be sure it is
the same world. And if
not, what power is there to make it
reappear (wind
is not a substance or
your breath on the mirror) the

picture you imagined,
come down to earth
like the angel in Tolstoy's story
to help you tie your shoes. A
child walks out the door you locked last night
and you hear yourself asking the time
in an empty house. It is

so important. Something to fill that
foot or so of space you're afraid
to leave. Why is it possible
to imitate almost anything but
oneself, the distance that listens
and has no answer? Because you dream at night
you are naïve

from *Other Names for the Heart*

and nameless. Your helpless throat
drinks dust among sparrows.
Pretty soon, you say, pretty soon
I will look at you out of eyes
that have learned, in exile, how to fetch
things back, from that space between
a world I had composed

and this one which breaks me. Is it
that serious? Your
shadow like a pietà, limp in your arms
but carved hard in stone. There is
no voice at the center. But as
Ponge imagined it, "then the nocturnal
outcry reverberates", and

between your blood and nothing, in that space
where you were last seen alive
the mirror reforms, a fish swims at its edge
and amazes you. How many words does it take
to redeem one? The issue
is not love. That word is broken.
To wake up in the mountains, cold

with first snowfall, it could be memory
asking for food, a
child now adult gazing past herself into
the mirror of the wind, not lost
but patient. Your vision of being
at one with things is hard, not easy.
Your sense of being separate follows, it

resembles despair but can
still speak. When you leave
abruptly the door swings
like a body that can't decide

from *Other Names for the Heart*

which way is out
and must guess its direction. Like Yoko's eyes
in the snow story, the girl whose body fell

dead through the flaming house, beyond words
or love. Only her leg
moved slightly. That is the feeling of silence
the cry at the center (not voice)
no one hears. You melt with the snow,
just the slightest pressure.
He lifts you up and takes you to the window

naked, to look at the white world
to look at the mountains.
This is the end, the departure, your
self from self, your substance from the mirror.
Distance takes your hand, the train comes in
leaving a sound of breaking glass.
Then the mountains, only the mountains.

Her Seasons

Who you are not
is who you will never be

first the *breva*
then the fig
at different times
two different fruits
on the same tree

you are not like that

this figure cutting between two idling trucks
in a hurry to cross the road
disappears in someone's doorway
suddenly as the sun goes in
and the fig tree spreads its shadow over the earth
like a mind suddenly aware
it knows nothing at all

and that life changes
and you change, you change life
are not the same thing, the bird's
groin anoints, in
sunlight, her feathers
held by his beak, this
play of words between us

if we are to succeed

that which you are, becoming
what you are not
is not

quite possible

from *Other Names for the Heart*

likelihood
is the force of the sun
multiplied by every thing
its hands have touched
do you want it to be this way
you forget, you forget
who you are, what
doorway you go into
a ship's horn following you like the cry
of a bull from the harbor its
gigantic cranes at rest

and all that hair

that fine intelligence
wearing its bright skirt
like a banner against the indignity
of having to explain
the fig tree's double life
its twice-bearing, twice-born
replica of the first fruit

this is not your life

the southern Mediterranean city
filled with otherness
streets of shadow, streets of sun
time hidden, time
deepening in gardens

it lifts us like smoke
over the green hedges of our birthplace
until we touch our first beds
and find them unmade

from *Other Names for the Heart*

Other Names for the Heart

This feebleness, this trembling
at the edge of self. Robert

Schumann suffered fits
of shivering, apprehensions of death.

Fear of high places. Fear of all
metal instruments including keys.

The note A sounding always in his ears
later became voices. His

piano returned to the silence of wood.
The air that gave him music

reverted to air. Wind, and rain on the window.

What do you listen for? The earth
is wounded. Earth cannot make you whole.

Spirits of the old
earth return, yes, they
linger and confuse you. Yet we are bodies

and sometimes, when the light is good
we move as music, we compose ourselves
in patterns of exact time

and dance as blood to blood, the piano
silent, the melody only in ourselves.

But it takes the courage of gods
and we are human. It requires

from *Other Names for the Heart*

what our eyes refuse to see
to see ourselves, as Schumann
dragged from the icy river, the Rhine
in February, quite insane

saw or
felt himself that night
breaking the surface, the cold flow
of time his hands had touched so masterfully.

Other names for the heart, all
obsessional, like the heart itself

rise like bubbles of air
the breath we keep or lose. Some boatmen

found him and pulled him to shore.
What they rescued was a question answered.

from *Other Names for the Heart*

Cante Hondo

At eighty-two her great artery
broke in the old woman. She
fell and they laid her out
on the white reddening bed.

Now after the funeral
the mattress and sheets are piled
at the back of the house.
Tomorrow

he will take them into the field
and light a match.
He will burn the blood of his mother.
No one else can do this.

from *Other Names for the Heart*

Words for Orpheus

Now that you have become she
your face her face
your body hers

the change almost complete
the distance grows until it becomes
pure presence
but without

the details presence had
not needing to be remembered
as now

memory tries
and tries too hard
like a dog circling its permanent ache
for a place
to lie comfortably

I at my own heels
tread too close to recognize
the half of my body she left me

in the near total calm
of the cold November sun
struggle to get up
try to get back

to the meaning of this pattern of sheer loss
the words the voice changed
thin now, nerves only almost

from *Other Names for the Heart*

to imagine a new face
perfect as an icon, but colorless
imprinted on air
which is the future's walls

always receding, always there
they take no shadow
they make no claim but

patience
which is not a virtue now
it being too much
a circling back
to what is impossible

that the voice chanting in the firelight
was the voice of a singer
and now the leaves will wait until

the first frost
which has touched us both already
changing the meanings of words
we learnt together

that grew too familiar
that became finally the bones
of an older love we had only borrowed
for a while
which we fleshed with ourselves

and now, how you have changed
how she has become that distance
that separates me from the critical sky

where the past walks in glory
backwards, like an omen in reverse

from *Other Names for the Heart*

its hands outstretched to touch
something I cannot see
which has no human features

no mask, no name
so bright is the overwhelming sun
that blinds me and makes my blood cold.

Premonition

She kicks off her jewelled sandals.
The rain will wash her feet.
The long hair of the rain
will hide her eyes. Any moment
the way is lost and must be looked for
without footsteps, the gaze
always the gaze, breaking
through heavy cloud. Wild animals
living the night through their eyes
as we live by fire, whisper
this is not the way. Turn east, turn west
plod north or glide to the south
it is all one where the spirit stands
barefooted in the rain
waiting. She gathers the young trees
and eats them leaf by leaf
drinking the rain. Blood collects
in the footprints she leaves behind.
On Broadway the lights flash out her name
a hundred years from now, the
wind that turns the rain-wheel
rises and dies, circling her feet.
She moves as a flute breathes
through all the stops and ghosts of air.
The lights flare in our bone-cells.
It rains as it never rained.

from *Figure of Eight*

Figure of Eight

"En la bendita soledad, tu sombra"
  —Antonio Machado, *Del Camino*

"That girl standing there" —W. B. Yeats

1

Frost a little like Yeats
a great poet no one wants to be
caught dead sounding like

and Pound might have got it wrong
but Lowell's excursions into history
were fruitless, mirrors just

to magnify the self
and diminish the anguish of time

What Pound suffered at last with the Jews
was incarceration and the threat of death
the wages of love, to survive this

but eventually the stories get told
yours, mine, in whispers or through
that silence which is terrifying

because it is "its own nothingness"
the gap in the journey that annihilates
the entire road. So far one goes

has gone, must come again
to where the pathway and the feet
are identical, and you are not

the figure lost or I the shadow left.

II

That afternoon
the rain came
riding the back of the wind
we watched, naked behind the screen
and couldn't make love, the wind and rain
did it for us, and you sang
a love song from your village
it moved in the wet air and rush
of water through leaves and grass
the trees shook their ankle bells
and flung their hands
"an unbroken continuity
of existence in itself"
to borrow words from Jean-Paul
who was as remote from that moment
as you are gone now
beyond the Manhattan skyline
city, city, the great divide
the "empty world of laughter" as you put it
to walk out in the lamplight
as the snow drifts down
a hundred years ago
an hour from now
"for the most beautiful girl in the world
can offer only what she has"
that circle of light in the dust
which Lakshman drew around Sita
to protect her from her story
the imperative of her own fate
the passion of rain falling
bent-headed into open hands
but she went back under the earth
and Rama grew tired of life
and crept to the river's edge
and vanished as a fish slips through its ring.

from *Figure of Eight*

III

While I was making coffee
this morning in October
a coral snake climbed up a dead ivy vine
to the window sill, its tongue alert
for early autumn insects

pretty the quick black eyes
I checked for holes in the screen
the fissures in my own skin
and watched it swing slowly from vine to vine
in a pattern remembered from dreams

repeating the dance figure
anchored at head or tail
of your feet on the boards of the stage
the lock and pivot somewhere in
the lifeline of the body

at points that varied, as a poet will
his rhythms, or a dancer's breath
then loosing its grip to fall
flat to the ground, its whole length
never the head first

a moment to recover
then the slow crawl, this cobra relative
through the skelter of ants at the wall's foot
like Pound in the tent at Pisa
to learn it all again

from memory to climb the sunlight
genius of beginnings with no ends, life
forever ahead of the sentence one reads
or creates, as
your body in repose, your body

from *Figure of Eight*

wanting our eyes wants more
breaking and saving the figure, the double
circle of time returning on itself
both snake and dancer
Patterning as did Yeats, or Frost the native

or as Lowell wanted, something too close
two bodies at bed in the heart
the earth-smell stronger than either
the beauty of nature in no way
comparable to that of art, which is its own end

(to paraphrase) and yours
pretty one, the kiss
between us this distance now
and "What is this separation?" you ask
the sunlight and October air

this nothing and all… Insect words
flit at the tip of my tongue, the dead
vine my lifeline even as I crawl
hungry into winter. Love
I eat my words, am filled with emptiness.

IV

They brought him hemlock and he
drank it like a snake
his dancer's mind accepted
the body was old and should go

and form was everything
form, the pattern, the artistry as it
touched on things and gave them shape
shape to live by, shape to die

from *Figure of Eight*

the thread through which the spirit moves
that breaks and remains the same
in the anguish of knowing
nothing lives up to itself
or can ever return

An old man falls into silence
having said everything
and finally "I was wrong, I was
mistaken"

but nothing can change that now
the enormous tragedy of the dream
is the form the body is left with
the pattern it leaves
                  is silence

and every voice that ever spoke
the sadness of your eyes in repose
the dark light of laughter there

after love and rain.

V

Do cries fall
in the category of silence
        the thought itself is enough
hidden away in a blood-cell
or a stone cell underground

how the body survives
what it knows is not the favourable air
of successful laughter, irony
of ironies, *iron maiden*

Osip Mandelstam
whose muse turned to hunger
in deep winter
        the cry the silence
edging into daylight like a spider
when the light fades

the one circled by nothing
the eye ringed by her admirers
the bride, her bachelors even
soledad

to live life to the hilt is such a
strange expression and must relate to
battle or murder, how
        else to draw the bull
onto your sword
who love that kind of dance
necesidad

which way do we go, what is the *tao*
who haven't phoned or will not phone
so long or write a simple note
or send it

if we are nothing and must create ourselves
as the wind creates deserts, trees
and gardens, excuse enough
        the tuft of inky hair
        soft where my fingers enter, make
the rain-dance

is memory
bitten tongues and words lost
in the wet silk of open mouths
commingling, dry by morning

from *Figure of Eight*

how to be clear without confusing
issues which are forever confused
by definition, so
                wild the silence, its cries
of ecstasy, its unbound hair
the poet searching his garbage heap
sweating and freezing

"that beauty may be
in small, dry things"
an antidote to all this dampness
like a laundry line
                the Indian cotton print
torn beyond wear
washed and kept as a keepsake
vanidad

What gathers here
has no way out.
I open my hand and release
the invisible thing with wings.
I release you, your shadow is heavy.
The *mudras* change, your hands make
"a woman becoming two birds".
You are out there now somewhere.

                VI

My mother goes out one door
My father the other

the stage is empty, the theatre
is full of invisible eyes
nothing moves

from *Figure of Eight*

tungsten bears the silence
the light, well past the melting point
of human nerves

tension, at the point where lovers
break and separate
and the children continue to wait

watching that last place
where the two cast their last shadow
the invisible door that opened once and

closed… The way you look for
is not the way. We are free to choose
what is visible, visibly ours

the thing in hand, the captive.
When the sun falls in just such a way
on that yellow stucco wall

something that flies away and hides itself
and later calls long distance
teases you with yourself. Your

being, your not being there
is the closest to touch I can come.

VII

Ill fate and abundant wine.
    —Ezra Pound

The lives of fragments. This pathetic duty
to pick things up and put them back
where they belong. To tidy
the edges of life

from *Figure of Eight*

so the centre is clear, the circle where
you alone stand witness
to an orderliness which is forever
breaking and scattering in its own helplessness
what you love and protect with your life
or things simply gathered, how
to tell them apart, your
self from each one.
                Dumb things without mouths
that shine in their quiet pleading to be kept
a little longer.
            I sent the box by freight
five working days to the tenth floor
New York address. The pink towel, the small
tape recorder, a *Norton Anthology*
some school notes and ball-point pens, the old
leather sandals… miscellaneous things
from the past now coming to crowd you.
I kept the little copper bell
that fell off the anklet, I keep
too much to myself, I take, misplace
things where they are not. They dance
a silent pattern on the carpet in the shadowy house
singing under their breath
so only the blood can hear it. As
my father would whisper her name
while he went about his carpentry
or stood at the sink rinsing things
over and over until we took them from him.
Summer too long where is fall the keen
Canadian wind
the clear streambeds of eyes, the
lassitude of honey.
             Means and ends
"The honey of peace in old poems"
the clear viscosity clouded by the cold
of living fragments.

from *Figure of Eight*

              Why should the agèd
men, old men
should be
beautiful manners
                    a life for a life
for a time, picked apart like Penelope's threads
so the figure can return whole
in the mirror of the silent telephone
the unforgettable voice
at some number listed somewhere in the sky
of its lights at night
                    The box is sent
filled with oddments… a photograph
someone took of you in bed
who loved you but never touched you
as these words attempt to keep that touch
the wind knows and is expert at,
no human.

VIII

Not enough to speak the language of one's time
there is no such thing. Or to love
the lovers of one's days and nights
who are ghosts of others, who mourn
for you and for themselves.
                    The name of this one I speak
over and over in the air she left
behind her. Name me, name me too.

The peripeteia, the journey never over nor
long enough. On a rock at a point where the path
turns, she is sitting, her face averted
waiting, waiting for something…
mas Ella no faltará a la cita, the

from *Figure of Eight*

loss of others to others, or
the expert wind. The merest change of light.

Matsya, the fish, the first
to come, the first
to return, among
the incarnations if
the circle holds.
                      To know
the dancer from the dance, her hands
that make the shape of Krishna's flute
or fingering more intimate things in the ever
questioning never ending
city night, the bee
enters the flower, the flower
opens, and closes.
                      Name me, name me then.

Brahmins not eating fish or flesh
for they are the forms of creatures that God
has taken in time, though man
eats woman, woman man
and the tree spreads its shadow over all
the north wind brings cold rain
the cigarettes are empty
                      Name me then
as another. Its own nothingness
returns as a figure of speech, a
paper or bamboo bird hung from the curtain rod
in the window facing east, a tender
photo of a *geisha* with a paper fan
too young to know much
                      someone's child
about to become
another's girl. Name her for me now.

No more elegies, *no más*.
So far one goes the long way home and on.
The light has hands and turns itself
so slowly from frown to smile
the day latening towards the coast
in sunlight on a clear road with the tape-deck playing
the light back to you
                      the evening *raga* sung
in the raw voice of the sea
the three descending notes repeating
                      naming you again
asking you to return. And you are gone.

En la bendita soledad, tu sombra.
In the blessed solitude, your shadow also.

from *Figure of Eight*

Chinese White

When Trickster put on
a deer's vulva and lay with
the chief's son, he too
bore children. The well

now filled with bones
is dry, and empty of tears.
The tears are in the bones.

When they are born
there is still time for
seasons. Late summer becomes
a winter's child, and the ones born

in autumn come to life
in the spring. At two
the eldest one said
"Sometimes at night

when my eyes are open
my eyes make dirt move
to a silly place". My friend

who might have danced
for fame and money
is finding life difficult, and
there are no swans in Austin

no pools of carp
reflecting the human beginner.
In early winter, rain
is the pattern. Rain on grey grass.

from *Figure of Eight*

Save your girl children.
They will suffer
and bring great pain
before the sun goes down.

Primitive

In the singles bar
the Shulamite sings
her griefs, her wandering song
under the drugged artificial stars
that guide us home.

Never gave you enough credit for being
ordinary, the obvious, what we
live for. Not
the mountains, the long upland pastures
of sunlight and cloud. Heroes

above and below
the norms of love and being.
Awake in each other's arms we embrace
the emptiness elsewhere that keeps us
here where the journey began.

In the brain things go wrong.
What calls has fingers.
The bird just after dawn crying
scarlet, scarlet
in a nearby tree.

We have what we're not while it lasts.
A kitten born from an egg
with a snake's head, four human feet
curled together for warmth
before this first last sunrise.

Soleá

Grey squirrel
sits on a
tree limb, its
tail tucked over it
like a tent
under the rain

the eyes of a wild animal
can never close, the
future watches there
remembering itself as an eternity
of questions the light asks
the sound of a pencil dropping

in the leaves, the
infinite activity of
lying in wait, a guerilla
in Nicaragua
or a grey squirrel framed
in a window of square panes
one's life, one's life

the autumn rain
that ages what it touches
fur and silence, fur
beyond blood-heat the cold
of stroking air
the mission, always the mission
beyond one's life one's means

green leaf, pale rain
grey features of the wind
and in between, the peace where

from *Figure of Eight*

the thing itself lies still
withholds its life

at the target's very eye
where the self runs
in widening circles of asking
as if in some other life
these too would be its lives

the eye light
as a fallen pigeon feather
detached, patient, beyond desire
the green leaf nicked at the edge
by something that passed
too quickly to make sense

eye of the rain
heart-murmur, belly-whisper
precious skin, precise
surface of depth, touch
this, do not be afraid
your acids will erase it or
it turn to feed on you.

from *Figure of Eight*

Assia

If I am to stay where you put me
give this note to the one who was expecting me
a white ribbon tied in her hair
unravelling now. In the doorway of that

shop that is about to close
how to tell the difference, but for the eyes
concealing the knowledge of a lost property
as a light that is fading. Who

of her own dark generation having escaped
to live this long, who, of her wandering kind
solo now, the stage hers, weeps silently.

The woman who waits becomes
less and less visible. When night falls
she is the whole of darkness waiting to go.

Full Moon Story

> "¿Eres la sed o el agua en mi camino?
> Dime, virgen esquiva y compañera."
> —Antonio Machado, *Del Camino*

1

Mother, cradling the sky
in your loose blue sleeves
wind arrows the yellow wheat
forever, it seems, in one direction
and I walk behind you

You never turned
to ask me who I am
I am unidentified still
a man without identity, a
father without speech, words, for his daughters

And the water continues to flow
Kitaro, under Fujiyama
the owl, the tuk-too, flute-calls
peace, love, the innocence that is evil
the evil that is tolerable

because it is lovely.
I am free to write
my questionmark in your womb
curled, the foetus, as my hand lies
curled against your thigh

hoping for a second birth
the touch that failed, the touch that
flashed between us in late May
two people alone, each wanting
the lost half of the world in the other's body

from *Figure of Eight*

Chords of electronic wind
frenzy the bamboos by the mountain stream
the water's nipples rising
like raindrops, like small fish
nestlings cheeping for food

The music is over. The music is gone
with your song in the far distance
I think I can't reach. My clothes
smell of yesterday's bed
and today's carpets. The nerves

are steadier than they should be.
I am strong, strong
with the strength of the weak
who must stay still to survive
or of the very powerful

whose mere gestures can destroy.
I am the monster you gave birth to
so gladly. The one so full
of hunger even the stones
aren't safe. The music is over

and the wind returns
formless, inhuman. Give me back my name
to play with again. I
gather you in my arms. I gather
emptiness, as a dancer gathers eyes.

II

The heart is a chord
that must be played with care
or it unhappens.
Words that don't burn are no good.

from *Figure of Eight*

Truth seeks itself.
The melting and freezing sensation
between us, within us
leaves no room for comfort, no room

where the door opens on perpetual sunlight
or on twilight, the hour you're most
afraid of. In your hands
I am all things I have been

but the future resembles a bone
someone tossed in the grass
after a feast. I love you in your
freedom, but

as another woman said
"The absolute freedom of the human creature
is horrible." And beautiful too
in the pattern you make of it

the ever-open question. At Easter
the children insist on their candy
chocolate eggs and rabbits
beyond the age for such things. They were

mine to play with, now they play with me
as you play, the chord in me
that sings and burns. Over the hills
the whole city lies with you

in a deep sleep. It is too early to live.
Self, I whisper, self
how do I gather these fragments?
Her skin was always softer than my hand.

from *Figure of Eight*

III

At fifty a man should settle for less
than the whole
but that thing always burns
"The devil" he said, pointing to his crotch
what changes is what's happened
and the spaces between, the missing parts
can only resemble what's happened
though it is late the world is young

We talk all night and
go to bed in the cold
too tired to do it
The voice that sings in your dream reaches me
as whales communicate
in the elemental telepathy of the ocean

which is where we swim
seeking each other
Though by daylight the music has changed
syncopated with the clock
that watches us
        the hundred streams
shed by the sacred mountain
announce Manhattan and the perfume of
studios mad to get the least note right
before the light burns out

As in my nerves
the coffee spills
and leaves a bloodstain on the floor
your dress immaculate white
your eyes so dark there's no telling it is day

from *Figure of Eight*

This is love then
This is the body's time between
askings of touch, the bee
hovering above the half-open flower
myths of whatever gods, who never grow
old or tired
           what bird is that
you ask
calling in the valley, but

I must go
I must go, it is getting late
The truth is I have stayed too long
The truth is the truth, I
lose myself in you

I am angry for my lost self
I am angry with you

                IV

I touch your body in an animal's eyes
your hunger, your wariness
of this old encroachment, this

almost-trap of a different
harmless nearness. How can I erase

my shadow from the earth, live
as pure light, a thought
your hand needn't touch? My smell

circles me always, like holy fire.
Your smell belongs with the night

it breathes, it eats, it leaves no shadow behind.

from *Figure of Eight*

V

Mother or placenta-twin
lost at birth
whatever the verdict now.

I have grown old beyond the power of my hands
to bless or touch your body
as a lover would. Not true

not true. But yes
I think of you
this meaningless Easter, under a clouded sky

and a south wind. You dance for your own gods
create, preserve, destroy
your breath is their life

your gift. But where am I
this swirl of wind, this
snail-shell filled with dust
which is life's
abundant pattern? Man to man
the mirror I become in time

cracks and shatters. The world seen through glass
only resembles the world, we
cut so easily. A woman is old

is everything, and is always in her youth.
Your blue sleeves trail the sky across the earth
in the manner of wind, and I breathe

in joy, in anger. Today the Japanese wind
moves me as the colours blue and yellow.
The Indian wind in your eyes

from *Figure of Eight*

darkens this. Somewhere at the heart of it all
someone suffers, writhes, hangs limp
and comes to life in a dream

I can't imagine. It is the son
you will never have, the
god or lover your will asks for

never to be born, of you or anyone.

The animal that prowls in all our hearts
has no shape or name, but the silence of old wounds.

VI

The full moon speaks
a dead language
one round vowel
then silence

For nine months we've shared our grief
I want your happiness, the
seed the moon denies
she stares too long and hard
her synthesis can drive men mad

and make a woman selfish
a will too pure, as Yeats thought
to belong in the world.
The bamboo clacks and rustles in the wind
both grass and instrument

a perfect fit in the hand
a dancer who loves crowds, and with
one of the stubbornest roots, wandering
God knows where, under the hard moon.

from *Figure of Eight*

Kitaro, solitary of the mountain water
or Antonio Machado who lost her
when she was very young
and wandered his own river, talking to trees

full moon, full moon, my dancer
to release the animal in you and keep
also the pure intention

beggars that these words are

supplicants at the mother's torn hem.

from *Figure of Eight*

Baby Upside Down in a Light Snowfall

The ones we know and recognize
through the flame, they smile and are gone
before we can name them   As memory is
what otherwise we would forget
what cries for forgiveness.
The mouths   the tiny mouths of snow that burn us.
The white nails of our mothers playing us wildly angrily.

from *Child Eating Snow*

Blue Fur Hood

Here are my eyes. Almost all the mirrors
are gone from the house, what I see
wherever I look, is myself
multiplied, in all possible forms.

So, in the light snow falling, I think of you
and reach for the telephone, your voice
furred with air of unbroken animal time
inside the wind. My brother's death

meant winter all over again, the dark eyes there
this time, like holes in the snow, cooing of Inca doves
lost in white smoke. *Being dead is*

hard work I remember from one of the Duino
Elegies. And also, *Every angel is terrifying*
in your breath's voice, white across thin blue air.

Child Eating Snow

for my niece Sylvia

In the wilderness she
imagined she grew up in
there was this photograph
of a child eating snow.
Handfuls of years
back behind memory now
and not her face at all
the eyes different
like a bird's eyes
eaten out by the wind.

II

In the winter sun that year
her father was all bone. Slowly
he was turning white
like her shadow on the snow.
In her dreams she never saw the sun
but sometimes a vivid suffusing light
like a torch shone through water
reminding her
of the first cry
of her birth.

III

On the tenth of March
a door opened somewhere along the horizon.
Her father left her. His dark eyes
return at night, beyond the stars

behind the snowflake.
The bird cries again
Cry I can't imitate
No eyes it has

IV

The blue static of lights along the freeway
grows colder, turns warmer
turns to flame. *Snow*
is how mirrors looked
before I was born the old woman remembers.
The sun squats in the grass
like a dam-bear. It is brown like her father's eyes.
Silent, as a mouth stopped with snow
her memory of this picture.

V

She sits in her mother's shadow.
She is eating the snow from his face.
Winter whispered her name, summer will
sing it now. The
single bird's cry
is a forest of music of leaves.
But it is still winter she said.
It is still February in my hands.

VI

The day is at breakfast.
Things, things to do.
Will the clouds leave the windowpane?

from *Child Eating Snow*

She's skating on last year's ice.
Wings hover above her, soft
hunter's wings. *Falcon, soul
exiled among ravens, Father, your shadow.*
It is summer.
The sky is mother blue
in the winter she imagines
she will live in forever.

VII

The child is eating the snow.
Her hunger is her thirst
her thirst her hunger.
Her father dies, her mother is alive.
Between seasons she draws breath
like a creature in hiding, to survive
what might watch her too long
too intently for love. So
she whispers her own name
Bird, how old am I
How old
is the rain in the summer grass
beyond mercy   beyond memory
Bring it to me. Bring it now.

from *Child Eating Snow*

Poem Depending on Dashes

But here with winter about to begin
a cold whisper in the leaves
and the woods full of ghostly deer
hidden between cracks of sunlight, where
looking I see only my old self
in a still place, a posture of waiting
the gun, the loving fingers
of those old vanished habits we shared
one autumn, or was it ten—
before something or someone called you
but—and the words that come now
Love is to me that you
are the knife which I turn
within myself—re Kafka's
by accident I recall, more than chance
which is a touch different if only
less violent—here
in this house farthest from your life
but which I imagine I love
as I can imagine we loved
despite all that happened, death, death
and your death—
the leaves ask no questions, or the grass
lacking the thousand human mouths
that are born to cry and devour
what we are, what we were—
But I am what remains of the eyes we shared
the noises, winds, voices, smells
as if it were a single animal
haunting itself—the shed trees, the
stamped lights of houses along the road
back, always back to this—the leaves—
the sentence never finished

from *Child Eating Snow*

Old Teacher

There are too many unknowns in the equations
and white chalk on black can slip into negative
at any moment. Truly it is the reverse
of a line one might write to a lover or friend
and so little is new. It is these faces
that slowly turn back into names, that learn
or fail to learn his voice, so when his day ends
nothing stirs in the room but a neutral dust
waiting for moonlight when chalk comes alive
as a white dry thin song. It is then
after the erasure of all the numbers and signs
that the beauty of the whole becomes transparent
and too clear to describe. As in a rare dream
the perfect poem or that faint lost chord
comes suddenly to mind, and he must tell everyone
that he was their generation's promised saviour
wandering in no Holy Land but time
in exile from the eyes that cannot hear him
the mouths that spit on him that scream his name.

from *Solo with Grazing Deer*

Lamp

While I was dreaming inside my flame
the wind bit at the edges of my teeth
and I thought I could see in the dark—
it was your word against mine.

Though they had broken shattered pieced together
Dresden and Hiroshima
Coventry London Guernica
the shadows you left wouldn't move.

So in Robert Capa's photograph
of a street in Bilbao in 1936
eight women and men and a young girl
look up at the sky at where German bombers

are coming. So it might have been
a little before dawn when a boy not quite
one woke up in a white crib in Yokohama
and saw shadows cross the ceiling of his room

—the world had soft bones
and old and brittle bones
and from time to time the light falls
exactly where the body runs to hide.

Landscape

In autumn the silences grow loud.
The sounds become echoes.
I have been gone a long time, they
changed my number, the branch
I hung from has been cut.
In the room the shadow dolls
play across bare walls, there are
fresh spiders. The music I heard came
from outdoors, celebrations of air, wind
rain, at the ear's edges, listening.
Why won't you come in? A traffic
of handcars running along rails over
loose coals. An engine starting stops
abruptly. The silence is like a brush across
dry canvas, like slow fingers playing
through pubic hair. A white cat sits
like a harp on the window sill. It is
cold in the mountains, after a summer
training my eyes to see
what they once remembered. I note
the place where my chair stood
a square of pale light on the grey
carpet. What would you like to do?
The soup kitchen, the popular *sushi* bar
usually fill by noon. The river
below is the colour and chill
of fish, my fingers go numb
winding and unwinding this wet string.
You used to play an elegant piano.
Now in the place where the piano was
a crowd of echoes cries circling
desperately to find your hands. We are
out of touch. A sudden dash of rain

from *Solo with Grazing Deer*

wets the glass and moves on. Tires
in the street exhale through wet teeth.
You were impatient with me. Three
seasons out of four the room chose colours
we both liked, heights of canyons brushed
with a first snow, brown shadowed by deep
green in the conifers just before dawn.
The patch of shadow where night
lay still in your armpit, a smell
like riverweed a moment out of water.
The almost white room is
emptying now. It is a book with blank pages
or a book whose familiar pages have faded
to this. There is no eloquence like
whiteness and silence. There are no
words where words end. The
room is empty now and white with shadows.
Black forest against white mountains
far away. A lone crow flying.

Blue Roofs

Antlers of white cloud
high to the north.
Bands of winter.

I remember one thing I should not
have forgotten. White times two,
an absence of mind.

Thinking to understand what cost her
her life, abstractions
of distance now, haiku

spelling their way from the sun
into my open hand,
rain snow snow

beginnings of blue.
Somewhere, how,
the bones gather to sing

in an empty ashtray, a deep well,
this lessening of hunger
as the years become sufficient

to themselves. Or am I saying
that white must be perfection,
a clean plate, a light without a source

the failure to remember your smell
a hiding of every colour
memory crying for water.

from *Solo with Grazing Deer*

Caravans

The weather is old.
Feathers of words drift
between rains, time
of Ovid watching the Black Sea

wanting home. But that
was his story. The rain
lifts, and someone's face
is watching you, still

for just this moment
without expression, like the sea's edge
where children were playing
only yesterday. Ships

came and went
carrying messages the rain
dissolved. Forgive me, they read.
I am penitent, let me return.

Years pass, but never completely
lose us. Pass like ancient skirts
of dancing bears and caravans
in the mud between rains. Death

was fire and the rains
extinguished it. Never
exile when your own shadow falls
foot by mile by plot along

the weather's old roads.
The words were harsh feathers
that scratched at your throat
in the dust between rains. Dry

from Solo with Grazing Deer

not tears. No grief
like old grief settled deep
under the stony earth, deeper than
where rains can loosen it. Bodies
not names. Not histories where
the letters get lost or misread
in lives which were fires until
the rains extinguished them. The

bright skirts and the caravans
passing. The poet crying for his mother
tongue at the sea's edge, not
lost, but found. Between

rains a face you never saw before
watching you try to recognize
yourself. The mirror at the sea's edge
between rains lifts its eyes.

from *Solo with Grazing Deer*

Railroad Tracks, House for Sale and Clouds

She left us while the light was bad.
A sudden movement on the hill, pepper
shaken from heavy clouds.

Someone kept asking, who?
But in a voice I didn't understand
like rain in a dry field, remotest echo.

The sweep of the long field slightly uphill
framed by two eucalyptus in the midground.
SEVENDE ESTACASA. Silence of afternoon.

And the tracks long long ago abandoned.
Grey deliberate rails from left to right
and back again, the eye the only pilgrim.

From left to right and back again
across the high, brown, dry sun-tipped grass.
Like her mind, like that dead tree.

Or the other one fallen on the roof
too frail to break the tiles, or the hill line
beyond, where we saw her move.

And the clouds darkening now,
the fire at their edges softer, gone.
Snow in the Andes. Hail on the lower fields.

How memory brings us to a place
then hides like that, leaving not even a name.
I call and hear nothing but holes.

from *Solo with Grazing Deer*

The Intimacy of Distance

Someone mentioned the *intimacy of distance*
as if we knew what it meant, how
far I have to go to feel
how close you are.
                    But that isn't
what he had in mind. The farther away
the place you long for where you have never been
the deeper inside you it grows
like a human child. But that
was not his point either.
                    To love someone he said
you must be content to imagine her.
But to love in that way
is to circle forever the cold point in the eye
at the centre that sees all things but itself.
                    He could have meant
there is no satisfaction comes to hand
that the hand can keep. It breaks
like a caught bird, soars, returns to the sky
as a mere colour for air.
                    Say blue, say grey.
And yes it vanishes.
And I remember why.

Solo with Grazing Deer

Granddaughter

Starting to crawl, she noses to earth
like a mole, it is too hard for her.
She must lie waiting like a seed
until spring when the earth is softer.
No, she is an animal she
Can't wait. No says yes and the
arms brace hard and her fingers
dig deeper, the carpet is a field
at night filled with hidden dangers
hunters, shadows, cries. And later
in dreams she will relive this
slow flight through exile, from the
first dark that would claim her again
if it could, straining now
toward the faint horizon of human voices
calling her home, asking her
where have you been, we've waited
a long time, tell us
what it was like back there.

from *Solo with Grazing Deer*

Apples and Apples

When she was a girl in Palestine
a soldier made her promises.

The wind off the sea
was a hand caressing her back—

inland the windblown sand
bit deep as bone.

I came upon her early.
She came upon me late.

Or put it another way, she had
lived more, longer, passionately afraid

where I was timid. Seven years between us.
Seven planets, seven stones smeared with blood.

We were both wanderers. But
she'd had to learn to live in ways

where I was innocent, death
in Europe had been real. For her

the subterfuge of languages.
For me the words we shared.

Too early and too late
can't average out as just in time.

Apples and apples. A door open
is always just closing.

No joy there now, no grief.
Fierce numbers feed the stars.

from Solo with Grazing Deer

Nocturne

House like a restless sleeper
shifts here
             settles there
suddenly
doors don't fit

Mother swift feeding her young
drops too far down the chimney
                 out the flue
flits from room to room
                wall window door
fighting the dark
a fact
brushing a dream

Awake now
now not
image of arctic sun
            all night
around the eye's horizon
circling

              animal
gentle or fierce
pure wonder
              in this house
fitted to my bones

Through trees the follow-through
of night wind asking birds
            hello the screech owl calls
closer to time

from *Solo with Grazing Deer*

far wheels driving hard
around dangerous curves
             the old road
         even at this hour
who's coming home
Father why are you
waiting for me
             your train left
almost thirty years ago
on rails of fire
             in winter
ashes to earth
where mother went first

Tomorrow a blank page
tonight a poem
the furnace where seeds of words
             melt and cry
wanting lives
wanting mouths

to kiss
to speak
             I breathe
grateful to hear the birds.

from *Solo with Grazing Deer*

Answers

What is the time of day
listening in a stone
warmed in an old woman's hand
on a concrete bench
in a square in an old town

a name older than mine
though grass drifts in the air
at the same instant I hear
the wind blow her skirt from black to shadow
like weather changing

when we return from war
when they returned from wars
the garden was always there waiting
though the postcards have turned brown
a dog's jaw buried to help

corn or alfalfa grow
a superhighway crosses the bridge
that connects time as it joins
both shores that long ago were one
was it her dog her garden

her son who didn't return
is she Dolores or Maria or
Kristen Helen Angelique
waiting for the sun to marry the wind
like weather turning

a name older than the town
an older name than any town
the square the fountain named for who

from *Solo with Grazing Deer*

first put it there
no clock heard anywhere
to what lover she gave birth
who drank her wine and left her dry
the wind to blow it all away
as footsteps up the rocky path
the stone drops from my hand.

Departures

They hung
stations from her eyelids
with real trains—
Anna, or
whoever takes her place.

Across the wind-darkened harbour water
white sails. Mud and rain
tracked in on children's feet.
Where, where have you been?

The lonesome train of her heavy century
long gone. Explosions still to come.
For me, a silence
in my ears, a winter
haiku—

Shimogyō ya
yuki tsumu ue no
yoru no ame

> *In the lower town*
> *across the heaped-up snow,*
> *whisper of night rain*

One is so frail.
Two are hardly better.
They were jackhammering the street outside
a day before the news came.

I like to think the snow
will give her back her shadow.
Milk across darkening grass, the cold.
Daphne gone to tree,
doe-ears flicking.

from *Solo with Grazing Deer*

Spring 2001

Where was there what time
Is where we begin…
Collect again what scattered

come, go, came, went
an order of verbs
too close to the fingertips
slips out is gone

fragment of a Mediterranean coastline
with blue-white villas   on sand
behind the closed concession stand
a pair of shoes
left waiting   it's no go

out of humour
out of touch

and comes the spring wind
a time for booking journeys
making time
walk ahead on its own feet

warm-green smell soft wind
confusion of waking dreams
lost in some city   gone
if our voices weren't
angry   time

bad and good
in whichever order
my sister, we
survivors, old ones now
ourselves

from *Solo with Grazing Deer*

we, us
taught her 35-year-old parrot
to sing the "Ave Maria" along with her
the sweet and raw voice
mingling   confused in the sun
where was there
that time

March-month   I was your son
I know your wind
that strip of gentle coast where others
always lived   paper, sand

the scattered pieces
I collect
myself.

Solo with Grazing Deer

Mother's son, father's son.
Late spring, the rain hangs on
like lost sleep.

A smell of fresh soap
when the wind drops. In the field below
a horse neighs. The wet cedars

bend to earth, looking for their roots.
Waxwings tilt and soften
the grey air between branches.

Memories still to come
like waves that haven't yet happened
gazing out across the wall of sea

to where the sea ends. The deer
gone. Myself I've been saying goodbye to
all my life. Beads of rain

like a series of clear names
run together. One, then a
thousand. Then the whole sea boiling.

Index of First Lines

A man's incandescent skeleton between my eye and the sun	42
All day a wolf has chased the sun	33
Always suspect the stranger	77
Antlers of white cloud	132
As dream corrects	40
At eighty-two her great artery	91
At night or just before dawn	64
At the tip of my gun the groundhog sits	23
Banded together again	73
Between midnight and daybreak	68
But here with winter about to begin	127
Chief Seattle never knew	41
Densities: a summer in the country	71
desert fingers	44
Do you hear this my friend	47
For the Sangre de Cristos	56
Frost a little like Yeats	96
God broke upon this upturned field; trees	12
Grey squirrel	111
He comes in the night between us	50
Headlights in the mirror on a lonely road	43
Here are my eyes. Almost all the mirrors	123
hero must break with his mother, be	61
His look, they said	60
House like a restless sleeper	139
I buried the dead	55
I have built you	51
I visited your grave	54
I was born within you	69
If I am to stay where you put me	113
If in your confusion	82
In a time of mock funerals and	53
In autumn the silences grow loud	130
In February the blind man walked in his maple wood	34
In the absence of father or god	52
In the singles bar	110
In the wilderness she	124
In this sea I find a lake	16

Kawabata talked about	84
Mother, cradling the sky	114
Mother's son, father's son	146
Now that you have become she	92
She kicks off her jewelled sandals	95
She left us while the light was bad	135
Someone mentioned the intimacy of distance	136
Somewhere	65
Starting to crawl, she noses to earth	137
The airfield stretches its cantilever wings	29
the candle fixed in a black room	59
The cure as with a flower is to water the root	75
The dark table where my ancestors ate	79
The dry wind ticks in the leaves	49
The ones we know and recognize	122
The pinecone's whorled	30
The sinewy nerves of a cabbage now	14
The threeday blow	26
The top of your head is still open	55
The weather is old	133
Then seeing it was still alive	78
There are too many unknowns in the equations	128
There is no equality among those	65
These four lie on a blanket	25
They had crucified a woman	37
They hung	143
This feebleness, this trembling	89
To have reached this state	36
To see it all fresh	67
To the trees at the waterline	27
We come into a new time; the heavymooned	17
What had become of the young shark?	19
What is the time of day	141
When she was a girl in Palestine	138
When Trickster put on	108
Where there were houses there is grass	81
Where was there what time	144
While I was dreaming inside my flame	129
Who brought from the snowwrecked	11
Who you are not	87

Index of First Lines

www.ingramcontent.com/pod-product-compliance
Lightning Source LLC
Chambersburg PA
CBHW031149160426
43193CB00008B/310